WRITERS' WORKSHOP SERIES

How to teach poetry writing at key stage 1

MICHAELA MORGAN

David Fulton Publishers

David Fulton Publishers Ltd
The Chiswick Centre, 414 Chiswick High Road, London W4 5TF

www.fultonpublishers.co.uk

First published 2003

British Library Publication Data
A catalogue record for this book is available from the British Library

ISBN 1-85346-918-1

Also available in the **Writers' Workshop Series:**

How to teach writing across the curriculum at key stage 1 by Sue Palmer   ISBN 1-85346-919-X
How to teach story writing at key stage 1 by Pie Corbett   ISBN 1-85346-916-5

Cover design by Phil Barker
Illustrations by Martin Cater
Cover photograph by John Redman
Designed and typeset by FiSH Books, London
Printed in Great Britain by Bell and Bain Ltd, Glasgow

Contents

Acknowledgements

The publishers would like to thank the staff and pupils of Roskear School, Cambourne, for their help in arranging the photo shoot at which the picture on the cover of this book was taken.

Acknowledgements are also due to the following copyright holders for permission to reproduce their material:

John Johnson (Author's Agent) Ltd, for 'Ruinous Rhymes – Pussycat, Pussycat', by Max Fatchen;

John Agard, for 'Hopaloo Kangaroo';

June Crebbin, for 'The Robin', from *The Jungle Sale* (Viking Kestrel, 1988);

John Cotton, for 'Silent . . .';

PFD on behalf of Roger McGough for 'Lucky' (first published by Puffin).

Every effort has been made to trace copyright holders, but in some instances this has not been possible. The publishers would like to apologise for any errors or omissions in this list, and would be grateful to be advised of any corrections which should be made to future editions of this book.

Dedicated to the children and teachers throughout the country who have tried these workshops.

Writers' Workshop

Poetry should above all be a pleasure – a pleasure to hear, a pleasure to say, a pleasure to invent. Most young children are fortunate enough to have some knowledge of verse – nursery rhymes, chants, skipping rhymes, advertising jingles, action rhymes and songs. These are the foundations on which we can build.

At this stage I feel the emphasis in poetry teaching should be on listening, speaking – joining in with the words, actions or rhythms and extending known rhymes. For this reason I have included several poems to share, both traditional and contemporary.

A Poetry Workshop does not *have* to lead to actual writing. Listening, speaking, honing the ear, enjoying the sounds of words and rhythm are important in themselves.

Writing poetry at this early stage is more successful as a group or whole-class activity with teacher or poet as scribe. This releases children from the mechanics of writing, and allows them greater freedom in composing, imagining, finding strong words and images.

I include some writing frames in this book and recommend that they be used as whole class or group frames – modelling the process of writing. Some children may move on to using the frames individually.

Making a start

Listening to and enjoying poetry is the essential first step

Reading a poem immediately before a break or to start or finish the day will not eat into your time and will help hone the ear and increase the breadth of acquaintance with poetry. The book or an enlarged copy of the individual poem used should be readily available for those who want to reread the day's poem.

Encourage children to find favourite poems and say or read them aloud to you, the class or each other. Enjoy the music of language as well as its meaning.

Oral and traditional poetry

Make an effort to build up a store of verse and develop familiarity with traditional chants. Titles of useful collections are given in the bibliography but do not forget to use the children and their friends and families as a resource. If you teach children who speak other languages than English make a special effort to include their rhymes and chants. Joining in with verse is not only for the younger children.

Practise honing the ear and all the senses

From time to time, take a few moments to listen or stand and stare. Ask the class to say what you and they can see, hear or touch or smell, and try to find a descriptive word or a simile to capture these observations. Complete silence in the classroom is necessary for the listening time. Silence is 'when you hear things'. Note the smallest of noises – also what you can imagine you hear, taste (e.g. I hear a ticking, *tick tick tick – the clock? or the teacher's pen? or my brain clicking as it thinks?*). Teachers should join in this activity – to be seen quietly concentrating, scribbling, crossing out and so on provides a good role model – and you will enjoy the activity.

Making a word hoard and writing together

Gather words and ideas in a whole-class or group session. Jot down all suggestions on a flip chart or board, and link words which go together because of their rhyme, alliteration and so on. Compose whole-class poems together. Sometimes, take existing poems and omit words or phrases. Discuss which would be good words or phrases to insert.

Reading aloud

To really enjoy a poem, it should be read aloud. Read aloud poems and verses on a regular basis. From time to time miss out a rhyming word or line, giving the children a chance to call it out – gradually they will learn entire poems

Reading aloud is an excellent chance to hear how/if the poem is working. This is a chance to consider making changes to poems written in class. The plenary is an excellent opportunity to hear rough drafts, applaud them and consider revisions.

Poetry as reading material

Poetry, with its patterning, its repetitions and rhythms, makes wonderful early reading material. Poems can contain stories told very economically. They can be learned with relative ease, shared and said together. They benefit from repetition. Never be afraid of reading the same poem over and over again. Sometimes just read it to enjoy the sounds and the rhythms – sometimes use it as a springboard to an activity or an investigation of patterns or sounds or feelings.

Redrafting and revising

The first writing of a poem is a beginning. Changes and improvements can be made. Do whole-class or group redrafting sessions on whole-class poems. Demonstrate the process of crossing out and changing, discussing reasons for the changes. Things to consider here are: deleting unnecessary words; changing words for more powerful or onomatopoeic or alliterative ones; tightening rhythm or rhyme; altering word order to put emphasis on important words or to avoid having to stretch for a rhyme; punctuating.

Being more specific and detailed can help a poem. Instead of 'we sat under a tree' consider what sort of tree. *'We sat under the willow'*, or *'we sat under the oak'*?

Revising a poem is less painful than redrafting a story. Writing poetry encourages experimentation with word choice, word order and so on.

Making a collection

Making a class anthology is an enjoyable activity which gives 'ownership' of the poems. You can choose a theme or poetic form or just allow children to find any poem that they particularly like. They copy out their poem (or key it in). Copying a poem sharpens the understanding of the poem. You often notice much more about a piece when you have to write it exactly as the poet has written it. Why is that punctuation there? Why is the line broken here?

Each child can read his or her chosen poem aloud and try to explain what they like about it. Illustrating the poem can help to make it more memorable and personal. Some children could learn their poem 'by heart'. The heart is a good place to keep a poem.

Making a tape

To accompany the class collection, record children reading verses – individually or in groups.

Invite a poet

Consider inviting a poet to school. Try for a poet whose work you have enjoyed – approach him or her through the publisher, through your local Arts organisation, local bookshops, the Book Trust (*www.booktrusted*) or the University of Reading, Reading and Language Information Centre website (*www.ralic.reading.ac.uk/lfa/*). The children can then hear a poem in the poet's voice and talk about it. Perhaps the poet will run a workshop or sign copies of his or her books. Prepare for the visit and follow it up. Allow children who can to buy copies of the books – to make the poems their own. If this is difficult, you should ensure the poems are bought and available to all in the library or classroom.

Tools of the trade

Equip the classroom with the tools of the trade – a rhyming dictionary, thesaurus and above all a large selection of books of verse and poetry including rhyming and unrhyming poetry, classic and contemporary.

And finally...

Why write poetry?

We do not necessarily expect all the children we teach to become poets but, by immersing them in poetry, we are making them aware of words, developing their language skills, helping them to become sensitive to imagery and feelings.

The skills involved in writing poetry are transferable to all types of writing. All writing benefits from careful selection of words, detail, keen observation, use of the senses, thoughtfulness and awareness. Word games and verse hone specific writing skills.

Poetry requires revisions and redraftings. All writers, particularly young ones, are often downhearted at revising longer pieces of writing. The brevity and focus of poetry makes redrafting appealing, achievable and fun.

Poetry is playful – it encourages experimentation.

A to Z of Poetry

A

Acrostic

A very popular poetic form in schools. The title of the poem (e.g. 'Holiday') is written vertically and provides the initial for each line.

H
O
L
I
D
A
Y

If you are going to write an acrostic, do some examples as a whole-class activity first and demonstrate the gathering of ideas before writing each line. Consider what makes a holiday, for example: resting, lying in bed late, sunny days, ice cream and lollies, taking it easy . . . . Then try to include some of the things you want to say in the acrostic.

**Happiness is our hope
On our holidays.
Lying in bed all day,
Idling, lazing, dreaming
Dozing...
All the time in the world
Yes!**

Advertisement poem

Advertising agencies think very carefully about their ads. Some of them have poetic qualities (rhyme, rhythm, alliteration and onomatopoeia are particularly popular devices). Look at advertisements, then try writing ones to tempt the reader to eat oranges, go swimming, read a book and so on.

Alliteration

Words beginning with the same sound (not necessarily the same letter – as in *'free phone'* or *'one wonderful wombat'*). Used frequently and to enormous effect by the Anglo-Saxons, alliteration remains widely used today in poetry and song. It is an effective way of binding words together and

making music with words (see Workshop 7: Monster Meals).

Alphabet poem

The well-known alphabet chant

**ABCDEFG
HIJKLM
NO
PQ
RSTU
VWXYZ**

is a valuable introduction and reinforcement of the letter names and order. Add a final line (*nod your head/go to bed/that's what I said*) for added fun and variety.

To write an alphabetical poem, you can take a subject and write an A to Z of it, for example, take 'CAT' as your subject; your poem could be composed of just adjectives:

**athletic, balletic, cosy cat.
daring, energetic, furry cat.**

or verbs:

**I am Cat.
I attack, I bite, I curl, I dance...**

(See also Workshop 7: Monster Meals for another approach linking in with alliteration.)

Ambiguity

Deliberate ambiguity – an excellent device in poetry. Unintentional ambiguity (*the secretary went down to the kitchen and brought up her dinner*) can have quite a different effect.

Assonance

Subtler than rhyming, it is a repetition of sounds to make a half rhyme (e.g. *crying time*).

B

Ballad

The Robin Hood Ballads or *Sir Patrick Spens* are examples of traditional ballads. They tell a story in a regular, usually four-lined (quatrain) form with a regular rhyme scheme (usually *ab ba*). A modern example of a ballad is 'Timothy Winters' by Charles Causley.

Brainstorming

When brainstorming for words, accept all offerings and note them. Then select from those submitted, giving reasons for your choice (e.g. *'This has a sharp sound'* or *'I like the alliteration here'*).

C

Calligram

The formation of the letters, or the font, represents something of the word's meaning (e.g. **SHOUT!** or *whisper*). See Workshop 6: All Join In.

Cinquain

Five lines and a total of 22 syllables, in the sequence 2, 4, 6, 8, 2.

Concrete poem

Also known as Shape poem. The layout of the poem takes the shape of the subject. See Workshop 8: Chips.

Confidence

An essential! Try not to be tempted into decrying even 'silly', 'rude' or 'nonsense' suggestions during brainstorming times. Out of mischief creativity can creep. Nonsense is to be valued – if not always used. Acknowledge successful poems – or lines or even words. Be tactful with revision suggestions.

Joining in with saying poems will increase speaking confidence, and writing poems as a whole class will increase writing confidence. The writing frames also provide helpful support.

Conversational

Many poems (most) are in a particular poet's voice as if the poet is having a conversation with you. Read Michael Rosen's work for examples of poems which capture rhythms and vocabulary of everyday language, situations and conversation.

Couplet

Two consecutive rhyming lines.

D

Dialogue

Don't forget that dialogue can be included in poems: in fact, entire poems have been made of dialogue. Try *Ghosts* by Kit Wright in *Rabbiting On* (published by Young Lions).

Diary poem

Try a diary of a goldfish – plenty of scope for repetition, refrain and changing word order to make slight differences!

E

Elegy

A lament, usually for the loss or death of someone. Try an elegy to a favourite teddy bear or to a lost sock

Empathy

To stand in the shoes of someone else, and to imagine and write how it would feel. Poetry taps into the imagination, creativity and empathy of human beings in a way that transcends anything you can target in the National Literacy Strategy.

Epic

A long story or poem of heroic endeavour. Not to be seriously attempted in class unless you have a year or two, perhaps a decade, to spare!

Epitaph

An attempt to sum up a life in a few words. They usually start with *'Here lies...'* You will find a wealth of them in *The Faber Book of Epigrams and Epitaphs*, where you will note that they are often used to humorous or critical effect, and many use wordplay for that effect. The Earl of Rochester's epitaph on King Charles II is fairly typical:

> **Here lies our Sovereign Lord, the King,**
> **Whose word no man relies on;**
> **Who never said a foolish thing,**
> **Nor ever did a wise one.**

Probably best attempted as the summation of the life of a typical figure representing a profession (e.g. teacher, Ofsted Inspector) rather than an individual. They can be cruel, as in one I prepared earlier:

> **Here lies a footballer**
> **whistle blown on his last game.**
> **He kicked the bucket, not the ball,**
> **and was never seen again.**

F

Figurative language

Use of simile, metaphor and similar devices.

Free verse

Verse freed from the need to rhyme or to have regular rhythm. See Workshops 10: The Poem Hunt, and 9: The Robin.

Form

Providing a form for writers to follow can act as a release and a starting point for writing – but feel free to adapt the form. It should be a supporting framework, not a straitjacket.

G

Have a GO!

Poetry is all around us and is one thing everyone can have a go at. Even those who 'don't like writing' can love poetry – though they may not know it. Anyone who can enjoy wordplay in jokes. Anyone who enjoys rhythm and sound in music. Anyone like this can write a poem – and enjoy it!

H

Haiku

A traditional Japanese form of poem which encourages the careful choice of words, economy and an awareness of syllables. Every word counts in a haiku. Every line break has to be carefully considered. A very brief form, it can help jolt a writer away from usual rhythms, pounding rhymes and well-used vocabulary. It is an exercise in making careful choices with language.

A haiku always has 17 syllables. It consists of three lines only. Line one has five syllables, line two has seven and the third and last line has five. A brief moment in time is captured in a clear visual image.

I

Idiom

Everyday figures of speech.

Images

Use of language to capture or create an image or picture.

Internal rhyme

Internal rhyme – rhyme within the line, as in *You peel and you grapple with orange or apple.* Internal rhyme can be within a word – as in *hubbub.*

J

Jokes

Jokes and wordplay alert us to language. Jokes can rely on puns, homophones or spoonerisms for their effect. They, and tongue-twisters too, are little steps towards poetry. See Workshop 11: Playing Around.

K

Kenning

Found in Norse and Old English poetry similar to a riddle, as the thing described is not named but described in compound expressions, usually of two words (e.g. *fast forgetter, ankle-biter*).

L

Limerick

A light-hearted exercise best done as a group or class activity. The finest examples are probably those of Edward Lear. The famed *Anon.* also produces a remarkably large quantity of limericks!

Line breaks

The place where one line ends and another begins. Children often need a lot of practice in this. Scribe nursery rhymes and well-known verses for the class – demonstrating where the line breaks are.

Write a well-known nursery rhyme or verse without the line breaks. Discuss where it would be good to break the poem and then rewrite with the appropriate line breaks. Do this from time to time to help develop some understanding of line breaks.

List poem (also **Thin poem!**)

Think of a subject and list its qualities

> **Christmas is . . .**
> **Dark nights**
> **Bright lights**
> **Rising hopes**
> **. . . and so on.**

If you keep to a carefully controlled number of words on each line you have a **Thin poem** too!

Possible subjects: *The contents of my head are...; In my pencil case.*

Encourage children to include unexpected, witty or well-described things in their lists.

Literacy Hour

Poetry fits wonderfully into the Literacy Hour. A whole poem rather than an extract from a book can be read as a starting point. Writing can be a whole-class, group or individual activity, and the plenary time is a perfect opportunity to read aloud, perform, listen attentively, applaud, and consider revisions and improvements.

M

Metaphor

A figure of speech in which one thing is said to be another.

Monologue

A poem can be written as a monologue – one person, or one animal, or one object talking.

N

Narrative

A narrative poem tells a story.

Near rhyme

Near or half rhymes can give a wider choice and subtler effect than full rhymes. (e.g. *summer/dimmer*).

Nonsense

Nonsense poems are wonderfully liberating. I suggest 'Jabberwocky' by Lewis Carroll, who invented portmanteau words in this *tour de force* – and anything by Spike Milligan.

O

Observation poem

Based on observation. Take the time to stand and stare – to really look, hear, taste...

Onomatopoeia

An interesting word in itself! Made up of two Greek words for 'name' and 'make'. Words, like *hiss* that make the sound they are describing are onomatopoeic. See Workshop 6: All Join In.

Oral poetry

Children will be acquainted with a range of oral poetry that they can be reminded of – jingles, playing songs, nursery rhymes. All poetry was once oral – epics and ballads were composed as poetry to make them more memorable before writing became widespread. The oral tradition continues strongly today. See Worshop 1: Rhyme Time.

Oxymoron

Apparent contradiction, as in *bitter-sweet* or *gloomily gambolling.*

P

Personification

Language that gives non-human things and objects human emotions or attributes (e.g. *The trees drooped with sadness...*).

Poem

A poem is many, many things, some of them contradictory. It can be direct – a quick connection to the heart, the memories, the senses. It can be indirect, subtly hinting. It can be moving, mysterious, sad, serious, comic, crazy, funny. It can be downright nonsense. It can explode. It can whisper. You can join in and clap and sing, or whisper it softly in your own quiet mind.

Coleridge defined a poem as 'the best words in the best order'. Wordsworth described his work as 'a selection of the real language of men in a state of vivid sensation'. In a poem, language is used with awareness, but should be real. Pope's famous adage 'What oft was said but ne'er so well expressed' sums it up. It's not just what you say but how you say it. Poetry is generally (but not necessarily) economical with language. The main thing – it is a source of delight!

Practical!

Poetry provides the opportunity for close inspection of a text. It is ideal for focus on an aspect of language – a grammar point, punctuation, a spelling pattern. I have seen a teacher making a spelling point memorable by the use of **Rap**. Copying or writing out completed work encourages care with presentation. Poetry is obviously much more than this – but its practical possibilities should not be overlooked.

Q

Question-and-answer poem

Ask everyone to write a question (a wide-ranging one such as *What is the sun?*). Then try to answer the questions – not factually!

Quatrain

A four-line stanza.

R

Rap

A type of performance poem that features regular rhyme, strong rhythm and fast pace. Children enjoy them because they are so full of life and contemporary in feel.

Redrafting and revising

Understandably, many children find revising unappealing and difficult, but it is essential. They have to be trained to do it. Whole-class poems can be the object of whole-class redrafting sessions. In this way children see the redrafting process modelled for them.

Repeat and refrain

Having a repeated refrain in a poem can help to bind it together.

Rhyme

Reading poetry of all sorts will demonstrate that it doesn't have to rhyme. That said, rhyme does have an enormous attraction. *But* if you are in danger of being forced into writing something pointless or silly, something that breaks the mood or lets the poem down – abandon the rhyme. The poem should say what we want it to say – rhyme is an extra. See Workshops 8: The Robin, and 9: The Poem Hunt.

Rhymes for remembering

There's the classic 'Alphabet Song' or '30 Days Hath September', 'I before E except after C' – rhymes help us to remember. Use the well-known rhymes and make up your own.

Rhythm

All poetry has some sort of rhythm – which is not to say it necessarily has a regular thumping rhythm. Familiarise children with rhythm by encouraging them to tap out a strong rhythm with their fingertips. You may occasionally let them loose with percussion instruments to really drive the rhythm home! Children could discuss which instrument best represents the mood of the poem. Sometimes an irregular, subtle rhythm or cadence is much more suitable to the mood of a poem.

Riddles

A great tradition spanning *The Exeter Book* (Old English poetry) to the *Beano*.

W. H. Auden memorably wrote that 'one of the elements of poetry is the riddle. You do not call a spade a spade.' See Workshop 12: Playing Around.

S

Senses

Using sensory description will enliven poetry and prose. Children need to practise noticing with all their senses and finding words to capture what they have experienced. See Workshop 10: The Poem Hunt.

Draw a hand. On each finger write one of the senses – to help children remember the five senses.

Take an object into the class (e.g. a piece of fruit, or a sweet). Ask for descriptions using each of the senses. Rework and revise the whole-class description. When refining the descriptions consider alternative words, putting in line breaks to make a whole-class poem.

Shape poem (see also Concrete poem)

In a shape or concrete poem the layout of the words reflect the subject. See Workshop 4: Chips.

Simile

One thing is described as being like (or as) another. See Workshop 10: The Poem Hunt.

Stanza

The approved word to use for 'verse'!

Syllables

Tapping out syllables/beats in well-known words (e.g. *classroom, playground, book*) or children's names can help children gain a concrete understanding.

T

Thin poem

Also known as **List poem**. One word or two words per line – set an arbitrary limit and stick to it.

Tanka

An extended form of Haiku comprising five lines in 5, 7, 5, 7 and 7 syllables. It is a word picture similar to a Haiku but its extended form means it can also contain some story element.

U

Understanding

'But what does it *Mean*?' Sometimes you cannot explain the meaning of a poem. That's part of the point of poetry – it has meanings behind and beyond its initial meaning. Sometimes, just let a poem wash over you – don't try to understand it, just enjoy the sounds, the mood. The understanding of it might creep up on you bit by bit over time. Sometimes there is no meaning – it is rhythm and sound, nonsense and magic.

V

Verse

Often used to mean *stanza* (as in 'the poem has four verses') but properly used to mean something slightly less than poetry. I write verse and sometimes I write poetry – sometimes my writing has the higher attributes of poetry – sometimes it has the rhyme, rhythm and so on associated with poetry, but it is of a lesser order.

Voice

Poems gain strength from being written in the poet's particular voice – the poet's own individual way of expressing himself or herself with words, images and language that is real and rooted in the poet's own life. Allow children to use their everyday language within their poems. Poetry should not be kept on a pedestal.

W

Wordplay

Free the mind, focus on a skill or start the creative process by playing a wordgame. Excellent ideas may be found in *Word Games* by Sandy Brownjohn

and Janet Whitaker (published by Hodder & Stoughton).

Writing frame

I have provided some for you, or you can make your own by taking a poem and blanking out a word or words, a line, a simile. Do a line from time to time just as a quick activity. Take 'I wandered lonely as a cloud' and try as

I_____ lonely as a_____.

X

Excitement! Exultation! Exhilaration! Exclamations! and now... Exiting from the need to find something beginning with X.

Y

Yes! Yippee and Yabbadabadoo! Feeling positive... feeling confident... having fun with words... writing a poem with...

Z

Zest and Zip and ZING!

NLS links

Reception

Key concepts:
Nursery and modern rhymes, chants and action verses:
- poetry with predictable structures and patterned language;
- verses including own names, rhyme and analogy – making rhymes from word families supplied, initial sounds – alliteration and tongue-twisters.

The workshops help to fulfil many of the requirements of the Literacy Strategy, particularly the following:
  To understand and be able to rhyme through:

- recognising, exploring and working with rhyming patterns, e.g. learning nursery rhymes;
- extending these patterns by analogy, generating new and invented words in speech and spelling;
- to use experience of stories, poems and simple recounts as a basis for independent writing, e.g. re-telling, substitution, extension and through shared composition with adults.

Year 1

Key concepts: as for reception plus rhymes with predictable and repetitive patterns – from a range of cultures, poems on similar themes:

- exploring and playing with rhyming patterns;
- generating rhyming strings;
- using rhymes and patterned stories as models for their own writing;
- substituting and extending patterns from reading through language play, e.g. by using same lines and introducing new words, extending rhyming or alliterative patterns, adding further rhyming words, lines.

Year 2

Key concepts: as previous plus poems from a range of cultures, poems by significant children's poets, language play:

- to collect class and individual favourite poems for class anthologies, participate in reading aloud;
- to discuss meanings of words and phrases that create humour and sound effects in poetry, e.g. nonsense poems, tongue-twisters, riddles, to classify poems into simple types and make anthologies;
- to use humorous verse as a structure for children to write their own by adaptation, mimicry or substitution; to invent own riddles language puzzles, jokes, nonsense sentences etc., write tongue-twisters or alliterative sentences, select words with care, re-reading and listening to their effect.

Year 3

Key concepts: as previous plus poems based on observation and the senses, shape poems, oral and performance poetry from different cultures, humorous poetry that plays with language – puns, riddles:

- distinguish between rhyming and non-rhyming poetry and comment on the effect of layout;
- invent calligrams and a range of shape poems, selecting appropriate words and careful presentation;
- choose and prepare poems for performance, identifying appropriate expression, tone, volume, use of voice and other sounds;
- write new or extended verses for performance based on models of performance and oral poetry read;
- write poetry that uses sound to create effects, e.g. onomatopoeia, alliteration, distinctive rhythms;
- compose own poetic sentences using repetitive patterns, carefully selected sentences and imagery.

Rhyme Time

Counting out

Vizzery, vazzery, vozery vem,
Tizzary, tazzary, tozery, tem
Hiram, Jiram, cockrem, spirem,
Poplar, rolling, gem

Inty, tinty, tethery, methery,
Bank for over, Dover, ding
Out goes YOU!

Eeny meeny mackaracka
Ero dominacka
ChickerBocker
Lollypopper
Om pom push
Out you must go.

Eenie Meenie Miney Mo
Catch a tiger by its toe
If it hollers let it go
Eenie Meenie Miney MO!

Ip dip my blue ship
bobbing on the water
like a cup and saucer
Out goes YOU!

Each Peach Pear Plum
Out Goes Tom Thumb
Tom Thumb won't do
So out goes YOU!

Rhyme Time

Speaking and Listening

- Enjoy saying the rhymes. Say one or several of the rhymes out aloud. Children can join in with the words.
- Ask children if they are familiar with any of these rhymes or if they know other rhymes.

They may know different versions of these rhymes. You may notice that in the 'Eenie Meenie' rhyme I have taken the less offensive option of 'Catch a tiger by its toe'. There is no 'correct' version of any of these rhymes. They vary from district to district, country to country and time to time. Many children may not have played with these rhymes at all but they may know television jingles. Accept advertising jingles as a modern-day version of playground chant if offered.

You will find many more traditional rhymes in the famous Opie collections (see bibliography). These rhymes are folk rhymes that have been used by generations of children for making choices or counting out. Their nonsense qualities seem to make them magical to children. Gathering these from the children makes the point that they already know a lot of poetry. Children can make it up. It is playful.

- Play with rhyme. Take a rhyming family word (e.g. *hop*) and ask children to come up with rhyming words.
- Collect counting out rhymes, playground rhymes and so on by asking children which ones they know – do their parents or grandparents know any?
- Make a cassette recording of them.
- Try to get rhymes from different cultures, other languages (there are some examples in the Opie collection, but it is better if the children or their friends and relatives can come up with their own).

Reading and Writing

- Write out a favourite rhyme on a large piece of paper, pointing to the words as everyone joins in.
- Read 'Each Peach Pear Plum' by Allan and Janet Ahlberg. This picture book uses the traditional rhyme as its starting point.

Further Work

- Use a counting out rhyme as an aid to choosing children for a particular task, leaving the classroom for break and so on. Use them in PE or at playtime.
- Make a collection of traditional rhymes.
- E-mail other schools in other parts of the country or in other countries to add to the collection.
- Take the first lines of some traditional chants that may not be known by the children and see if you can invent extra lines orally – nonsense is fine!
  Here are some to start with:

  Inky pinky ponky... (e.g. *My daddy had a donkey*)
  Etum peetum penny pie...
  Ickle ockle bluebottle...
  Ip dip...

- Use this frame to make up a class rhyme:

  Run and hop,

  _____.

  Jump and skip,

  _____.

  One, two, three,

  _____.

Action Time

Mrs Sprockett's Strange Machine

Mrs Sprockett has a strange machine.
It will thrill you through and through.
It's got wheels and springs and seven strings
And this is what they do.

Pull string number one . . .
. . . it begins to hum mmmmmmmmmmmmmm
Pull string number two . . .
. . . it goes Cock a Doodle Doo.
Pull string number three . . .
. . . it will buzz like a bee zzzzzzzzzzzzzz
Pull string number four . . .
. . . it will start to rrrrRRoarrrrrr.
Pull string number five . . .
. . . it will dip and dive.
Pull string number seven . . .
. . . it will fly up to heaven.

Mrs Sprockett has a strange machine.
It will thrill you through and through.
It's got wheels and springs and seven strings
And . . . I WISH I HAD ONE TOO!

Michaela Morgan

Action Time

Speaking and Listening

- Enlarge the poem to A3 size so that the whole class can see it.
- Enjoy saying the rhyme together.
- Work out suitable actions and make them as you chant the rhyme.
- Rehearse a performance, taking into account appropriate expression, volume, actions. Perform in different ways. Different children or groups of children could perform each string. The whole class makes the sound effects. Speaking aloud, taking turns, joining in, will all help children to gain confidence in speaking and being listened to. It will also help to develop a sense of rhythm.

Reading and Writing

- Enlarge the poem to A3 size so that all the class can see it.
- Use as reading practice.
- As a whole-class activity, using the writing frame, make up your own version of the rhyme. Some ideas:

String Number One – let's start the fun/it will fall on its bum/sing rumpty tum/tickle its tum.
Two – what will we do?/it will cry boo hoo hoo/whisper to you.
Three – it will climb up a tree/hop like a flea/sit on your knee.
Four – it will go out the door/fall on the floor/offer its paw.
Five – it will jump and jive/sit in a hive/call itself Clive.
Six – It will stir and mix/get in a fix/eat choccy bix.
Seven – go off to Devon/call itself Kevin/fly up to heaven.

Further Work

- Children can perform the rhyme in assembly.
- Children can illustrate or make a model of Mrs Sprocket's strange machine.
- They can make a cassette of their performance and a Big Book version of their rhyme.

- Further work can be built on the sounds 'm, r, oo' used in the rhyme.
- For a selection of other poems to join in with see the bibliography.

Mrs Sprockett's Strange Machine

Mrs Sprockett has a strange machine.
It will thrill you through and through.
It's got wheels and springs and seven strings
And this is what they do.

Pull string number one . . .

_____

Pull string number two . . .

_____

Pull string number three . . .

_____

Pull string number four...

_____

Pull string number five...

_____

Pull string number six...

_____

Pull string number seven...

_____

Mrs Sprockett has a strange machine.
It will thrill you through and through.
It's got wheels and springs and seven strings
And... I WISH I HAD ONE TOO!

Pussycat, Pussycat

Pussycat, Pussycat where have you been?

I've been to London to visit the Queen.

Pussycat, Pussycat what did you do there?

I frightened a little mouse under her chair.

(Anon., traditional version)

Pussycat, Pussycat where have you been?

Licking your lips with your whiskers so clean?

Pussycat, Pussycat, purring and pudgy,

Pussycat, Pussycat, WHERE IS OUR BUDGIE?

Max Fatchen

Pussycat, Pussycat

Speaking and Listening

- Enlarge the verses to A3 size so that the whole class can see them.
- Read the traditional rhyme aloud for enjoyment.
- Read alone, read all together and/or take parts, paying attention to appropriate expression and volume. Pay attention to the punctuation. Point out the question marks indicating questions and demonstrate a 'questioning' voice as opposed to the 'statement' voice.
- Ask children if they already knew the nursery rhyme.
- Encourage them to tell nursery rhymes they already know. The aim of this is to validate existing knowledge and to give the whole class the opportunity to become acquainted with popular rhymes. It also provides the opportunity of showing or making written versions of rhymes that the children largely know orally.
- Read the modern parody of 'Pussycat, Pussycat'. Explain that poets often take rhymes and add their own ideas to the original.

Reading and Writing

- **Use the writing frame.** As a whole-class activity complete the writing frame on p.24. Collect examples from the children, trim them to the right length and rhythm and scribe them. Some ideas for 'Pussycat' writing frame:

I frightened a tiger. I frightened a bear/I stood and I shivered in my underwear/I went to the shops and I went to the fair.

Further Work

- **Do similar work with other nursery rhymes.** 'Humpty Dumpty' and other well-known nursery rhymes provide excellent starting points. See Appendix for further examples of addled rhymes.
- **Make a class anthology.** On a large sheet of paper, record some of the rhymes remembered or generated. Over time, make a class Big Book Collection or a series of posters. The children can illustrate the books or posters. Read them

with the children from time to time and make the book or posters available for all to see at any time. Sing the songs and rhymes as the occasion arises. Extend and adapt the rhymes orally or in writing. For example:

Here We Go Round The Mulberry Bush
The Mulberry Bush,
The Mulberry Bush
Here We Go Round The Mulberry Bush
On a cold and frosty morning.

Change the weather depending on the day, e.g.:

On a bright and sunny morning/On a wet and rainy morning/On a dull and gloomy morning/ On a wild and windy morning.

Change activities to fit in with your current activity, e.g.:

This is the way we brush our hair/This is the way we tidy up/This is the way we make a line/This is the way we find our book.

Add children's names, e.g.:

This is the way Ben turns around...

The more you do this the more confident the children will become in their grasp of rhythm and rhyme.

More Addled Nursery Rhymes

Humpty Dumpty sat on a wall,
Eating black bananas.
Where do you think he put the skins?
Down the king's pyjamas.

(traditional)

All Purpose Nursery Rhyme by Michaela Morgan

Humpty Dumpty swallowed a fly,
lost his sheep, stuck his thumb in a pie,
jumped over the moon with the dish and the spoon
and then sang a lullaby.

Writing frame

Pussycat, Pussycat

Pussycat, Pussycat where have you been?

I've been to London to visit the Queen.

Pussycat, Pussycat what did you do there?

_____

Writing frame

Humpty Dumpty

Humpty Dumpty sat on a _____

_____

Humpty Dumpty had _____

_____

Hopaloo Kangaroo

If you can jigaloo
jigaloo
I can do the jigaloo too
for I'm the jiggiest
jigaloo kangaroo

jigaloo all night through
jigaloo all night through

If you can boogaloo
boogaloo
I can do the boogaloo too
for I'm the boogiest
boogaloo kangaroo

boogaloo all night through
boogaloo all night through

But bet you can't hopaloo
hopaloo
like I can do
for I'm the hoppiest
hopaloo kangaroo

hopaloo all night through
hopaloo all night through

Gonna show you steps
you never knew
and guess what, guys?
My baby in my pouch will
be dancing too.

John Agard

Can You Do The Kangaroo?

Speaking and Listening

- Enlarge the poem to A3 size so that the whole class can see it.
- Explain that the poet has started with real words – 'jig' and 'hop' (and arguably 'boogy') and played with them, making new words with them. We have *jig* (turned into *jigaloo* and *jiggiest*), *boogy* (*boogaloo* and *boogiest*), and *hop* (*hopalloo hoppiest*).
- Ask the children if they can think of other ways of moving – ask them to think of synonyms for move or walk. List the suggested words and add your own, e.g. *skip*

  > *bounce*
  > *zoom*
  > *bop*
  > *limp*
  > *slump*
  > *plod.*

Demonstrate the meaning of new verbs by making the movements.

Reading and Writing

- Read the poem again and, as a class, use the writing frame to make up a new stanza including one of the words collected.
- Photocopies of the writing frame can be given to the children to create their own individual stanza and illustration.

Further Work

- Perform the poem as a class, with individuals or groups performing their own new stanzas within the poem.
- Use in drama/movement classes.

Writing frame

Hopaloo Kangaroo

If you can _____

_____

I can do the _____ too

for I'm the _____

_____ kangaroo

_____ all night through

_____ all night through

Mrs Brown

Mrs Brown went to town
and what did she see?
She saw a cow
it said 'meeow'
so she took it home for tea.

Mrs Brown went to town
and what did she see?
She saw a cow
it said 'bow wow'
so she took it home for tea.

Mrs Brown went to town
and what did she see?
She saw a cow
it said 'Ker pow!'
so she took it home for tea.

Mrs Brown went to town
and what did she see?
She saw a cow
it said 'Oh wow!'
when she took it home for tea.

When Mrs Brown got back home
what did she see?
She saw cows in the bedroom
cows on the stairs
cows watching telly
cows in all the chairs
cows in the bath tub
cows in the hall
cows in the kitchen
and no tea left at all!

Michaela Morgan

Mrs Brown

Speaking and Listening

- Read the poem aloud to the class.
- Enlarge the poem so that everybody can now see it.
- Enjoy saying the poem together with appropriate pace and expression. Individual children or groups can be given parts.

Ask children to point out the rhymes.

Reading and Writing

- Use the enlarged poem as reading material.
- Think of other animals Mrs Brown could meet. List them and try to think of rhymes for the new animals.
- Some ideas: a chick/feeling sick, a pig in a silly wig, a sheep going beep beep, a lion whose name was Ryan, a horse in tomato sauce etc. . . .

As a whole class write additional verses using the writing frame.

Further Work

- Individual children, using the writing frame, can write and/or illustrate their own verse.
- A Big Book of Mrs Brown verses and illustrations can be made and used as a reading book.

Writing frame

Mrs Brown went to town

and what did she see?

She saw _____

_____

so she took it home for tea.

Words to whisper

Words to whisper...

Words to SHOUT.

To pack a punch!

To cast a doubt...

Words to relish

Words to chew.

Antique words

or words brand new.

Words to clacker and to clack

like trains that travel on a track.

Words to soothe, words to sigh

to shush and hush and lullaby.

Words to tickle or to tease

to murmur, hum or buzz like bees

Words like hubbub, splash and splutter

wiffle, waffle, murmur, mutter.

Words that babble like a stream.

Words to SNAP! when you feel mean.

Get lost! Drop dead! Take a hike!

Shut it! Beat it! On your bike!

Cruel words that taint and taunt.

Eerie words that howl and haunt.

Words with rhythm. Words with rhyme.

Words to make you feel just fine.

To clap your hands, tap your feet

or click your fingers to the beat

Words to make you grow – or cower.

Have you heard the word?

WORDPOWER!

Michaela Morgan

All Join In

Speaking and Listening

- Enlarge the poem to A3 size so that the whole class can see it.
- Read the poem aloud to the class – don't encourage children to join in at this stage. In your reading demonstrate the meaning of the words by your actions and tone of voice.
- Now discuss the meaning of the poem with the children and help them to understand the vocabulary. Less well-known words (e.g. 'cower') can be more easily demonstrated than explained.
- Explain the term 'onomatopoeia' (see A to Z of Poetry) and with the class pick out examples from the poem.
- Divide the class into groups to work on a performance of the poem. Encourage the children to shout the word 'SHOUT', whisper the word 'whisper', sigh the word 'sigh'.

Reading and Writing

- Collect other examples of onomatopoeic words for display.
- Make a display of some of these onomatopoeic words, written as calligrams.

Further Work

- Look at 'Fishes' Evening Song' (overleaf) as another poem featuring onomatopoeia. Mention can also be made of alliteration, but the main point is simply to enjoy saying the poem aloud.
- You could write a whole-class version of an animal song based on 'Fishes' Evening Song' (e.g. Owl or Lion or Snake Song).
  Some ideas:

  Owl's Evening Song/Too witt too whoo/oo oo/flap flutter/night sounds,
  soothing sounds/we waft our wings/as we perch/darkness falls/moon shines/shush shush hoot hoot/hush/eye glint/swoop swoop/whoop/ air rush/claw grabs/This we do.../too whit too whoooo . . .

- Read and perform a range of poems simply to enjoy the sounds of words. See Bibliography for suggested collections.

Fishes' Evening Song

Flip flop,
Flip flap,
Slip slap,
Lip lap;
Water sounds,
Soothing sounds.
We fan our fins
As we lie
Resting here
Eye to eye.
Water falls
Drop by drop,
Plip plop,
Drip drop,
Plink plunk,
Splash splish;
Fish fins fan,
Fish tails swish,
Swush, swash, swish.
This we wish...
Water cold,
Water clear,
Water smooth,
Just to soothe
Sleepy fish.

Dahlov Ipcar

Monster Meals

My monster eats:

shops that are shut,

a shed and a hut,

sheep and ships

and shark and chips!

Sh!

(By children in Year 2 Townlands School, Leicestershire)

Monster Meals

Speaking and Listening

- Enlarge the poem to A3 size so that the whole class can see it.
- Read aloud for enjoyment.
- Emphasise the 'sh' sounds while reading the poem.
- Ask the children to point out the 'sh' sounds.
- Emphasise the difference between 'sh' and 'ch' (e.g. ships and chips).
- Introduce and explain the term 'alliteration' (see A to Z of Poetry, p.7)
- Talk about the monster. It can eat anything. Encourage the children to make suggestions for things the monster can eat.

Reading and Writing

- Read the verse again and gather in ideas. As a whole-class activity make another poem – this time using a different initial sound or blend (e.g. 'ch'). Collect 'ch' words and list on a flip chart or similar, e.g.

chocolate, cheese, chips, chunks, chips, chimpanzees, charts, choice, chattering, choo choo, chew, church.

Try to arrange them in a poem – rhyming or non-rhyming, e.g.

> *My monster eats:*
> *chocolate chunks*
> *and chips and cheese*
> *chewy choo choos*
> *and chimpanzees.*

- Individual children could move on to writing a line or a verse of their own.

Further Work

- Do similar work with other sounds.
- You could also follow up by making similar verses using homonyms, e.g.

> *My monster eats:*
> *Pairs of pears*
> *And hairs of hares*
> *And bare bears*
> *And stairs that stare.*

- Collect and enjoy other food and monster poems (see bibliography).

Chips – a cut-up poem, or a shape/concrete poem

- Writing a poem such as this develops the skills of word selection and word ordering, redrafting and revising
- This workshop does not start with looking at a poem. It starts with trying to capture a word. The emphasis is on finding a good word – not making a sentence. There is an example poem at the end of the workshop which can be read in a plenary session along with the poem the children have produced.

- Cut out rectangles of thick paper or card to look like chips – big fat chips, skinny chips, long chips and so on.

Speaking and Listening

- Ask children to think of words to describe:
- the way chips look (e.g. *chunky, fat, thin, skinny, crinkled*)
- how they feel (*soggy, sticky, crispy*)
- how they taste (*salty, crispy, crunchy, soggy, vinegary*).

Reading and Writing

- Write words on individual chip shapes and stick up on flip chart/board/large card using sticky tape or Blue Tack.
- Use some of the chip shapes to keep as blanks and to write conjunctions, punctuation and so on.
- In discussion with the children move the words around.
- Try out the effect of different arrangements until you have made a poem.

As the words are easily moveable there should be no reluctance to experiment – omitting words, adding extra words, changing order of words, changing line breaks. Redrafting like this is probably more appealing than crossing out and changing.

Further Work

- Children, with their own chip shapes, can make up their own chip poem.
  Present the poem on a cardboard plate or cone shape (like rolled newspaper) and you have a shape poem.
- Look at the example poem provided and discuss.
- Write other shape poems featuring food, e.g. spaghetti and other pasta shapes, fruit.

Example Poem

The following (see opposite) was written by Class 2 (whole-class mixed Y1 and 2) with myself as scribe and workshop leader. When offered words I grouped them according to sound and we managed to find rhyming or half-rhyming words. This is by no means essential.

Chips!

Crunchy chips

Salty chips

Squeezy chips

And squidgy chips.

Wiggly chips

Vinegary chips

Curly chips

And crunchy chips

Spicy chips

Spiral chips

Smiley chips

And fat chips

Hot chips

Thin chips

Yummy in my tummy chips!

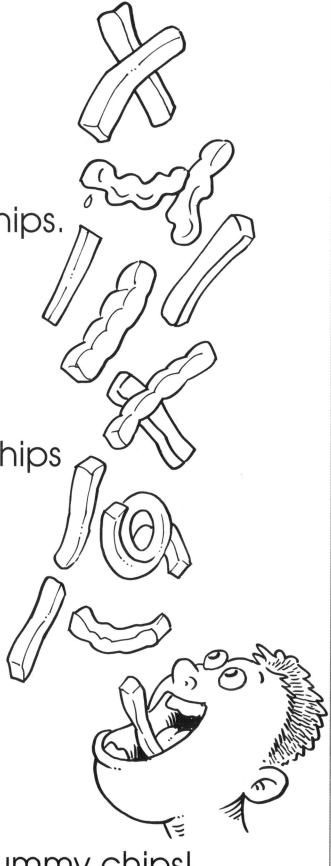

The Robin

I tried to write a poem today,
I tried to make it rhyme,
I tried to get the meaning right
But every single time
I thought I'd got the hang of it,
I thought I'd got it right,
I found I couldn't think of a word
To rhyme with bird
Or, that is, robin.

I didn't want to say
I saw a robin.
It was bobbing
Along and sobbing.
Because it wasn't.

So I started again.

Once, last winter, in the snow,
I was out in the garden
At the bird table,
When I turned round
And saw on the path beside me,
A robin.

It was so close
I could have touched it.
It took my breath away.

I have never forgotten
The red of it
And the white snow falling.

June Crebbin

The Robin

Speaking and Listening

- Read the poem aloud to the class without them joining in. This is a poem for one voice rather than group participation.
- Point out that many poems have a bouncy rhythm and the opportunity to join in but some are quieter, more thoughtful, and you can read them aloud with one voice or to yourself. Point out that some poems rhyme but rhyme is not necessary.
- Check that everyone has understood the poem.
- Enlarge the poem so that everybody can now see it.
- What difference would it make to a poem about a robin if it had to rhyme? It would become bouncier; the mood would be lost. The poet would not have been able to capture what she felt and what she had seen. Emphasise again that rhyming is not essential to poetry. Rhyming is fun and is sometimes right for a poem, but if it stops you saying/writing what you want to say, if it makes you write nonsense by *mistake*, start again – this time without rhyme.

Reading and Writing

- As a whole class or in groups, take an object and try to capture it in a non-rhyming description. One 'poetic sentence' will be a good start. Objects could be anything that might mean something to the class (e.g. a well-worn teddy bear, a prize they have won, a picture).
- Brainstorm words and ideas and scribe them on to a flip chart or a large sheet of paper.
- Look at the lines you have scribed for the children and try out different word orders, line breaks, different choices of words.

Further Work

- Link this workshop with the following workshop, 'Poem Hunt'.

The Poem Hunt

This workshop does not start with the hearing or reading of a poem. It starts with an exploration.

- First, remind the children of the five senses.
- Explain that a poet is like an explorer. He or she uses all their senses and tries to look at the world with open eyes, all senses on the alert – as if they have newly discovered the world.
- Go on a poem hunt to make poetic sentences. Take the worksheet out to the playground or around the school or use it on a school visit. Omit some senses if you feel the activity is too challenging for some. Smells are particularly challenging to capture and describe.
- You can add imagination to the list for some children (I imagine/I think/I feel/I dream) to try to capture mood.
- When the words and sentences have been captured, take the worksheets of rough notes back to the classroom to be rewritten and redrafted. Cutting out all unnecessary words and making changes will improve the description and make them more like a poem. It is important to do several whole-class redrafts to show the way. For example:

I see a tree
it is bent
like an old man   becomes

      I see a tree, bent like an old man.

I hear some other children
whispering to each other
like the wind   becomes

      I hear children, whispering like the wind.

I smell
the air
it's a nice fresh breeze   becomes

      I smell the fresh breezy air.

I touch a stone
it is warm
like a pet   becomes

      I touch a stone, warm as a pet   or
       I pet a stone, warm to my touch

- Now, or at a later date, ask each child to put all his or her 'poetic sentences' together to make a senses poem. Small changes can still be made to improve the poem. Words can be taken away or added:

I see a tree, bent like an old man.
I hear children, whispering like the wind.
I smell the fresh breezy air
and touch a stone, warm as a pet.

- Finally, think of a title.

Poem Hunt

I see a_____

it is [*describe it*]_____

it is like a_____

I hear a_____

it is [*describe it*]_____

it is like a_____

I smell a_____

it is [*describe it*]_____

it is like a_____

I touch a_____

it is [*describe it*]_____

it is like a_____

Word Hoard

In this workshop the focus is on collecting interesting words.

- Choose a topic and brainstorm all the words associated with it.

- Be sure to include some adjectives and verbs, not just lists of nouns.

- The following topics provide a starting point. Add your own topics to fit in with current weather, events, interest.

– Christmas

– Birthday

– Bonfire night/fireworks

– Snow

– Rain

– Snake

– Worms

– Other small creatures (e.g ants)

– Particular animals

– Activities (e.g. racing/running/football/ swimming)

Draw on the children's existing knowledge and encourage use of dictionaries and thesaurus.

- Make a list poem using a selection of the gathered words (*worms wriggle, worms wind, worms loop . . .*).

- Make a a shape poem – for example, use the words you have thought of for 'worm' to make a worm poem in the shape of a worm.

- Make a class thesaurus using the words you have gathered.

Playing Around

Word games are important for building confidence, honing skills, providing starting points and increasing awareness of language.

- Tongue-twisters are fun and useful for reinforcement of initial sounds, introduction to alliteration, word selection by sound, memorising and performing. Tongue-twisters need to be repeated a number of times – this is obviously helpful for early reading and for speech development. Children enjoy the challenge and the nonsense of tongue-twisters.

- Reading and writing riddles develops observation, consideration of language and a certain obliqueness which is a characteristic of poetry.

- Puns and jokes obviously amuse children (although younger children often laugh out of politeness and a wish to join in!) and I consider them to be small steps towards poetry. They involve thinking about language and understanding that one word can have more than one meaning. They develop an understanding of the way that a word can be used in different ways to different effect and enhance an enjoyment of language.

Tongue-twisters

Betty Botter bought a bit of butter.

But the bit of butter Betty Botter bought was bitter

So Betty Botter bought a bit of better butter

Red bug's blood, bed bug's blood

A thorn in the thumb makes a thin thumb thick

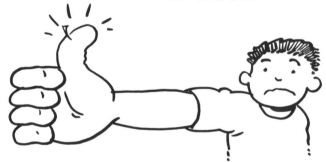

Swan swam over the sea

Swim swan swim

Swan swam back again

Well swum swan!

Tongue-twisters

Speaking and Listening

- Read the tongue-twisters aloud – individually/ as groups/as a class
- Invent class tongue-twisters orally – focusing on a sound you particularly want to introduce or consolidate.
- To reinforce knowledge of alphabet and alphabetical order you could invent or find a tongue-twister using each letter of the alphabet in turn (e.g. *Ann Anteater ate Andy Alligator's apples, so angry Andy Alligator ate Ann Anteater's ants. A big bug bit an old bold bald bear and the bald bold bear bled badly and blubbed, So . . .*).

Reading and Writing

- Invent and write whole-class and individual tongue-twisters.

Further Work

- Make individual or class collections of tongue-twisters.
- Individuals, groups or the whole class can write more tongue-twisters, using a dictionary to find additional words with the specified sound.

Tongue-twisters

Write a tongue-twister using 'D' sounds.

Here are some words to help:

dog, duck, dirty, den, deep, dark, dig, dingy, dug, dozen, dozy.

_____

_____

_____

_____

Riddles

Speaking and Listening

- Riddles are a very old and popular form of poetry. They are short and mysterious. They usually have no title – you have to guess what they are about.
- Read the riddles provided overleaf.
- Guess the answers.
- As a whole class discuss riddle descriptions you could give of the following:

kettle, balloon, ball, sun.

You will notice that certain characteristics apply to several of the subjects. For example the ball, balloon and sun are all round. The kettle and the sun both heat water. You can play with both a ball and a balloon. Both ball and balloon can be full of air. They could all be yellow or red.

- Make the point that when writing a riddle you have to think **very** carefully about the subject. You have to consider it more carefully than you normally would. This way of thinking is good practice for writing any sort of poetry. The writers also have to think of things to compare their subject with. This is good practice in thinking figuratively, using similes, metaphors and images.
- Read a selection of other riddles (see bibliography for recommended collections).

Reading and Writing

- As a whole class write one of the riddles you have discusssed. Consider the subject carefully. Scribe the class suggestions, making changes as you go. Model reading back and checking, considering and revising.
- Remember to write as if you are the subject (I am round. I bounce in the sky.).
- Keep it mysterious. If you are going to give a clear clue, save it for the end of the riddle!

The riddle description is usually short (but not necessarily so). It can rhyme but this again is not necessary.

Further Work

- Individual children can move on to write their own riddle which they can read out for the class to guess. Subjects could include everyday things you can see in the classroom or playground, animals, natural phenomena (shadows, water, fog, ice etc.).

Riddles

Each of the following riddles describes a punctuation mark. Can you guess what they are?

WHO AM I?

Am I a curl?

Am I a squiggle?

Where will you find me?

At the end of a riddle?

(question mark)

LOOK AT ME!

I stand up straight and tall

And balance on a ball!

Shock! Horror! Surprise!

You won't believe your eyes!

(exclamation mark)

STOP HERE

I help you with your writing.

I make the meaning clear.

I am small and round and useful.

I make you stop just here.

(full stop)

Riddles

Night Hunter by John Kitching

Some think that I am blind by day.

At night my sharp eyes seek out prey.

I haunt the woodlands with my song.

I'm wise. And smaller creatures know

   I'm strong.

Who? Who am I?

(owl)

Silent...by John Cotton

Silent, I invade cities,

Blur edges, confuse travellers,

My thumb smudging the light.

I drift from rivers

To loiter in early morning fields,

Until constable sun

Moves me on.

(mist)

Puns

A sailor went to sea, sea, sea

To see what he could see, see, see

But all that he did see, see, see

Was the bottom of the deep blue sea, sea, sea.

Bears bears everywhere.

I can see a bear in front

and I can see a bare behind!

Whether the weather be fine

or whether the weather be not

We'll weather the weather

whatever the whether

Whether we like it or not

I scream for ice cream!

We all scream for ice cream!

Puns

An understanding of puns usually relies on a knowledge of homonyms (words with the same spelling but a different meaning, such as *stamp, light, stick, fine, might, dear*) and homophones (words which sound the same but have a different spelling or meaning).

Speaking and Listening

Explore examples of these words (e.g. *jam* (for eating)/*jam* (in traffic), *stamp* (on a letter) *stamp* (on a foot), *eye/I, might/might, stick/stick, sea/see, hair/hare, deer/dear, bear/bare, stair/stare, whether/weather, saw/sore*).

Reading and Writing

- Enlarge the examples given for the children to read and enjoy.
- Check that they have understood the meaning.
- Meaning can be reinforced if the children illustrate or suggest illustrations for the words and verses.

Further Work

- Make a class collection of punny verse and punny words.
- Using some of the words given in the Speaking and Listening section above, work with children to write puns to add to the collection (e.g. *stamps*: Give me six stamps (*stamp foot six times*).
- Enjoy reading the following poem – 'On and On' by Roger McGough. Discuss the meanings and try writing extra stanzas together. Some expressions that may start you off are: *daybreak, sunset, catalogue, kitchen sink, rubber band, light bulb, dinner lady, giant sale, shooting stars, horse fly, clothes horse, battery hen, reindeer, buttercup, sunflower.*

On and on

Is a well-wisher
  someone
who wishes at a well?

Is a bad speller
  one
who casts a wicked spell?

Is a shop lifter
  a giant
who goes around lifting shops?

Is a popsinger
  someone
who sings and then pops?

Is a fly fisherman
  an angler
who fishes for flies?

Is an eye-opener
  a gadget
for opening eyes?

Is a night nurse
a nurse
who looks after the night?

Who puts it to bed
and then
turns off the light?

Is a big spender
a spendthrift
who is exceedingly big?

Is a pig farmer
really
a land-owning pig?

Does a baby-sitter
really
sit on tiny tots?

Is a pot-holer
a gunman
who shoots holes in pots?

Roger McGough

Display frames

Using the following pages for children to copy out
their final version of a poem will encourage them
to take extra care with presentation.

Bibliography

Oral and Traditional Verse

Iona Opie, *People in the Playground*, Oxford University Press.

Iona and Peter Opie, *Children's Games in Street and Playground*, Oxford University Press.

Iona and Peter Opie, *The Lore and Language of Schoolchildren*, Oxford University Press.

Iona and Peter Opie, *The Singing Game*, Oxford University Press.

Susan Hill (ed.), *Rhymes and Raps*, Eleanor Curtain Publishing (Australia).

Michael Rosen (ed.), *Inky Pinky Ponky*, Collins Lions.

Addled Nursery Rhymes

Max Fatchen, *Wry Rhymes for Troublesome Times*, Viking Kestrel.

Richard Edwards, *Nonsense Nursery Rhymes* Oxford University Press.

Poems to Perform

Michaela Morgan (ed.), *Words to Whisper Words to SHOUT*, Belitha Press.

John Foster (ed.), *Ready Steady Rap*, Oxford University Press.

Clive Sansom (ed.), *Speech Rhymes,* (A and C Black).

Paul Cookson (ed.), *Unzip Your Lips*, Macmillan.

General Collections

Paul Cookson (ed.), *The Works,* Macmillan.

Pie Corbett (ed.), *Poems for Year 3*, Macmillan.

June Crebbin (ed.), *The Puffin Book of Fantastic First Poems*, Puffin.

Read Me, A Poem a Day, Macmillan.

Poems Linked by Theme

Allan Ahlberg, *Friendly Matches Poems* (about football), Viking Kestrel.

David Orme, *'Ere We Go* (football poems), Macmillan.

Collections by John Foster, themes include: Sports, Ghosts, Space, Night, Snow, Sea, Shape, Food and many other, Oxford University Press.

John Foster (ed.), *Monster Poems* illustrated by Korky Paul, Oxford University Press.

John Foster (ed.), *Magic Poems,* illustrated by Korky Paul, Oxford University Press.

John Foster (ed.), *Pet Poems,* illustrated by Korky Paul, Oxford University Press.

Riddles, Puns, Jokes and Tongue-Twisters

Pie Corbett (ed.), *Footprints in the Butter and other mysteries, riddles and puzzles*, Belitha Press.

Brough Girling (ed.), *The Great Puffin Joke Dictionary*, Puffin.

Paul Cookson (ed.), *Tongue twisters and tonsil twizzlers*, Macmillan.

Paul Cookson (ed.), *Let's Twist Again, More Tongue Twisters and Tonsil Twizzlers*, Macmillan.